Limor Kohler | Anat Ben Natan

Israel Feeling at Home

10 Unique Interior Design Styles

Producer & International Distributor
eBookPro Publishing
www.ebook-pro.com

ISRAEL Feeling at Home
Limor Kohler | Anat Ben Natan

Contact: limoranat@gmail.com
ISBN:9789655751604

Cover: Interior Design by Hadar Aram. Photography by Shiran Carmel

Preface

...A moment before you dive in

This book would not have been published without the initiative of Anat Ben Natan, advertiser and businesswoman in the field of communications. Full of endeavors, she is a woman of action who sees no walls. She knocked on my computer screen one day and stated, "Let's meet." Conversations and ideas, her notions and mine about Israeli design, deadlines and correspondence - all came to life over the last two years and gave me the suitable framework to extract everything I had collected in my overflowing file of ideas, resting in the dark recesses of the computer. They would not have come to light without Anat.

Some people say: "Stop looking for a partner. Focus on your goals and rebuilding your life. The right person will eventually find his or her way to you." This is how I feel about meeting Anat.

Our thanks to silent partners Michal Vital and Liron Vardi, who remarked and illuminated; to Talia Tordjman-Weinstein, who helped focusing the spotlight on the world of design during the first years of Israel; to architect Eldad Soffer who, in our conversations, illuminated the previous decades; to Galit Edut for encouragement during the editing; and to all the people who encouraged us with their warm words along the way, were supportive and excited when we shared with them our doubts, conclusions and decisions.

To our families who left us alone during the weekends so we could start writing, collecting, shaping, filtering, moving and finalizing our dream without interruption - you deserve a decoration for valor for heroism.

Limor Kohler

Introduction

As in many other fields currently of interest to Israelis, interior design was not part of the establishment of the state. If for decades the word 'design' was uttered by people, it was used to designate the arts rather than home space. However, from the moment the notion of 'design' trickled into everyday life – first in small, measured steps inaccessible to the public, and later massively – it was a quasi-explosion all over. A breakthrough, if you wish. If you look at Israeli streets, you cannot help but noticing shops that are involved solely with design and styling. Even those that are involved with other areas take care to include some design items. Although designer shops have always existed, and some looked as if they were taken from a journal, the selling of design was not wide-spread. Only a few had adopted design; usually the wealthy, famous, trend setters or people connected to the world at large.

Being an elitist in general, it took a long time for interior design to reach the rest of the public, and it is still not on the agenda of the average household. Many people have a home that is 'neat,' 'attractive,' 'full of character,' or 'special' - the type that is based on architectural planning. The interior, however, does not necessarily express design planning of an entire system fulfilling residential criteria. Rather, it "resolves itself," according to the owner's taste or - in the same manner that many Israelis love to live their lives – by "going along with it." Whatever the owner considers attractive enters. Whatever works within the budget is included. Whatever was inherited or found in the street is welcome. The owners place everything as they see fit, and their homes look efficient and well-equipped. You can rely on them for that.

Interior design is defined in Wikipedia as "a specialized branch of architecture that deals with the planning and changing of interior spaces in structures. Up to the 20th century, it was one and the same profession, with interior design developing from within architecture. Contrary to architecture, interior design does not deal with the planning of entire structures, constructions and urban contexts, but rather with a detailed planning of interior spaces, addressing people's physical and psychological needs within built structures, public buildings and private homes. For example, the location and size of rooms in a house, lighting appropriate to various needs, and down to the smallest details of planning the kitchen cupboards." Over time, the meaning was also rendered to dressing the home, "home styling," as it has come to be called and interior design expanded to styles of design, usually imported from other countries - rustic, modern, ethnic, Nordic, Japanese, industrial, etc. Each style has its familiar features.

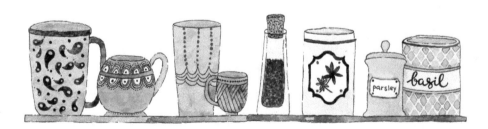

A multitude of cultures gathering in one country as a nation, just 70 years ago, made it difficult to form its own tradition.

As for Israeli design, can we find clear characteristics there? The question of Israeli design has been examined for years in architecture and design departments at universities. Many claim that there is no Israeli style; that interior designers and homeowners love to copy whatever they have seen abroad, in journals, on Pinterest or Instagram. Whatever someone has done there - can find a place of honor over here. There is a joke about the world of programming: In Israel, only one single software program was purchased. An Israeli bought a licensed program and all the other guys jumped on the bandwagon. Is this also the case with interior design?

Not necessarily. Although design ordinarily stems from an ancient tradition, Israelis could not count on an Israeli tradition simply because there was no such thing. A multitude of cultures gathering in one country as a nation, just 70 years ago, made it difficult to form its own tradition, and that is why another solution was found – counting on other styles.

Israelis love to break the rules, to reinvent themselves. Wherever there is a rule, it is likely that an Israeli will try to bend it, find loopholes, and create something irregular, almost like the Hebrew language itself, written in the Bible according to rules and with irregularities. And back to design: even if the home has a modern line, a Nordic style or Japanese elements, the Israeli designers will find their own way to stir and mix, coming up with a style that may have started with a known and familiar origin, but has developed into another style with their own personal and different statement, which is most likely not to be found elsewhere. To be more concrete: Eclecticism is the main trait of all Israeli design. No one wants to find himself fixated on one particular style, but rather desires gaining from all possible worlds. That is why one Israeli space contains Nordic and contemporary modern together with retro and some boho. It sounds like a mishmash but the result is harmonious. It works and it sells.

Eclecticism, one of the most prominent features of Israeli design, is not surprising. It is based on a wave rushing throughout the world in which eclecticism is its preferred mode of design. When we have Morocco, Italy, France, Scandinavian countries and others in the palm of our hand, both physically and mentally - with everyone becoming acquainted with the others' style by turning a page or tapping on the screen - inspirations mix and the products unite the global village into four home walls. Add to that the entrepreneur trait of many Israelis, their clear knowledge of what they want in their home, and the often-uttered statement "I did it all by myself" (even when assisted by a designer), and you will get the unique local mix.

Light, Openness and Simplicity

Beyond the fascinating mixture of styles, there are additional features noticeable in Israeli design which speaks a clean and simple language, one that any eye can understand. It is not complicated, cluttered or overflowing - even if the work behind it was extremely complex. The design styles reflect the typical Israeli personality; overt, talking about everything, hiding nothing, unashamed and proud of what exists, while living with enormous inner complexity. The sun sends warm yellow rays in the Israeli summer and winter, filtering natural Mediterranean sunlight into the homes, which cannot be found in cooler countries. Architects and interior designers fully exploit the climatic conditions by means of openings in the spaces which allow natural light in, while also enabling the outdoors to enter, at least in feeling. It does not matter whether the garden and its abundant flora face the calm blue Mediterranean Sea, or peeling rooftops with old and dusty solar water tanks, or even the neighbors' piercing eyes. Israelis are a transparency-loving people.

The inner structure of the home is based on the principles mentioned above, and when one looks at the designed spaces, one clearly notes a division into private and public areas, entrance locations, kitchen, exit to the garden, etc. Inside the home, a public area receives the guests with emphasis on a connected kitchen and a living room, enhancing the sense of size, airiness and openness. The bedrooms are concealed in the continuation of the home as one leaves the entrance area, since even the most open people deserve some privacy and intimacy. There is no staircase at the entrance nor is the kitchen hidden somewhere at the end; the living room has the largest window opening; and if the home is from the first years of the State - it is likely that a beam indicates where there was originally a porch, later opened in order to enlarge the space. Walls are undoubtedly superfluous in an Israeli home. Something, of course, should hold up the house or separate the private areas from the public ones, but Israelis will manage very well without the remaining walls.

After the planning of the structure we advance to the dressing of the home. The styles of design that you will find in this book were formed after Limor's infinite following of details and meticulously examining them on a daily basis - yielded by many years of experience in the written and digital media, as well as from her training as an interior designer, living and breathing the field. Although interior designers may call their style of design by names such as "modern with touches of vintage," "light rustic," or "eclectic Scandinavian" - a closer look presents shared elements. These elements are the ones that have created the new style definitions in this book, ranging from "Calculated Graphic Composition" and "Wild Wonderland" to "Nostalgic Grandma Chic" and "Cosmic Softness." It was surprising to find a space such as a living room containing a mixture of several styles together, or various spaces in the same home that may consist of different styles.

Eclecticism, one of the most prominent features of Israeli design, is not surprising.

Where Feelings Happen

The aim of this book is to map the innovative and current styles in Israel, in order to help the readers make a precise stylistic choice for their homes, while affording them a broad conceptual view. The definition of a style as rustic, modern, Nordic or industrial, seems too general. Although it provides a direction, it does not precisely clarify the effect one attempts to achieve - and in most cases, the definition stems from the homeowner's desire to convey a certain feeling: warm, pleasant, inviting, ascetic, etc. Rustic alone no longer represents a Tuscan or Transylvanian village, or a peasant's farm. The classic Nordic cannot remain within the cool boundaries of Scandinavia, but rather extends to an Israeli climate while adopting new features. Modern encompasses many facets - from cold minimalistic to heat-laden contemporary and industrial may be made of iron, leather and plenty of black color, but also play delicately with the boundaries of the light urban style. That is why we consider all the details of the pictures gathered in this book to be important, and the readers will be able to find here a more accurate style that suits them and their feelings as well as understand how to combine stylistic elements with the rest of the items in order to achieve the desired whole.

A final, and no less important, word about the appearance of the projects. The design detailed here pertains to its visual aspect and does not include structural planning. The breath-taking designs of Israeli interior designers that were chosen for this book are shown here because Israeli design is of high international standard. The choice of materials, colors and the visual language of all of the spaces that you will see on the following pages are a source of pride for our interior designers and their abilities. Each of them has adopted the touches of various worlds and turned them into their own language.

As far as this book is concerned - Israeli interior design is very much alive and thriving.

Where has
Israeli interior design
been hiding all these years?

I t has been busy surviving. Israel rose from the sands and built houses stone upon stone while having to deal with wars and attrition. It has had no time to deal with the esthetic side of life. At best, during moments of respite, its founders sat around a swamp soon to be drained, heating coffee from a little pot over an open fire and marveled at the migrating birds overhead.

"When architects who had studied and been educated in the European tradition came to Israel, they brought with them a European style, and planned structures as well as their interior," says Talia Tordjman-Weinstein, a multi-disciplinary designer and a lecturer for design. "The architect would do everything, from the macro level to the micro, but there was no official profession of interior design in Israel." She explains that the profession was first introduced into curricula only in the early 1980s, with the establishment of the Sadna College of Architecture and Design, a defining moment in the annals of interior design and architecture in Israel.

The early years of the young state which was declared its establishment in 1948 were characterized by simplicity and modesty, expressed in the homes as well. Only in the late 1960s was a turning point noted in the country, with the sense of euphoria and relative economic wellbeing following the Six-Day-War. Together with architecture, the notion of interior design began to trickle into awareness, and indigenous Arab elements as well as new American ones became noticeable.

The immigrants who have populated the country during its first years and before becoming a nation brought invaluable luggage from Europe and Middle-Eastern countries. Local artists dealt with the specific designing of furniture items. Most homes looked about the same; with the wooden radio, crystal ware, colored glass, long high-quality buffets, and local wooden furniture of Shomrat-Hazoreah, an Israeli kibbutz company founded at the end of the 1950s, or Danish Interiors (later known as Tollman's), founded by Jeff Tollman, a new immigrant who imported items from abroad. "The local impact became clear when Israelis started to go to Arab villages and towns to acquire straw furniture, embroideries, camel saddles, sheep-fur rugs, or rocket-parts that became decorative elements in the homes," says Tordjman-Weinstein.

Kitchens from the Regba Kitchens Co.
catalogue, 1970s.
Photo courtesy of Regba Company

The 70s have brought about the wallpaper, with its flowery or curving patterns, nowadays known as "loud," "psychedelic" or "retro".

Left: Midcentury Modern wood Chandelier
Right: Midcentury Modern Danish Secretary from the 60s
Photography: Amir Lahav

We encountered halls at the entrance, and many dividing walls, some even made of wood. Closed balconies extended from the living rooms. Balconies circled around the apartment from the living room to the bedrooms (no one thought it was a terrible waste of space). Toilets separated from the bathroom; kitchens with one line of cupboards on an elevated platform and an inner dining room in the same space. The telephone station had a place of honor in every home (who would have believed that today it has nearly disappeared), and the television, which appeared in the late 60s ,heralded the onset of the new Israeli tribal campfire, affecting the organization of the living room, making it the hub of the home.

The 70s have brought about the wallpaper, with its flowery or curving patterns, nowadays known as "loud," "psychedelic" or "retro." Along with geometric patterns in the bathrooms, stucco on the walls, wooden constructions of shelves, small food counters and kitchen islands influenced by the great America, and walls that made way for semi-walls. The Israelis have already known a thing or two about what was happening across the ocean, and allowed themselves to depart from their original conservative ways, starting to absorb influences from a lifestyle that slowly changed the home design as well. The living room grew in size, the television armchair took up a substantial volume, hosting turned the drink bar into almost obligatory, and plastic furniture dawned in the homes as part of the space age that induced rounded and amorphous patterns influenced by the first moon-landing that took place back then.

The 80s brought about an inflation of colorfulness, almost to the point of loud, with a creative abundance that did not always transmit regularity or a unified language in one space. Following that, the 90s showed signs of a budding eclecticism, with Israelis frequently jumping abroad and returning with scents of distinct styles from afar. It was about to become the new millennium that would mark the accelerated change, induced by the global village, technological innovations and recognition, although not a sweeping one, of the need for interior designers as a vital part of home planning or any other project.

In the recent years, we have witnessed a return of items from the 50s and 60s as well as interior features, in a quasi-nostalgic longing that retrieves the forgotten past, connecting to our grandparents' heritage from abroad, and conveying sparks of a grand past on to the center stage. If you wish, it is like living in the modern state-of-the-art without neglecting the feelings for yesteryear. Architect Eldad Soffer, who teaches interior design, was known to say, "Those years, as well as the 70s, now appear as a trend in interior design, especially in the realm of living room furniture and accessories. The simple lines are reminiscent of Scandinavian furniture, the turbulent patterns of fabric are produced more sensibly, and the items, dishes and lighting fixtures that appeared back then are returning with new technologies, while still echoing the 70s. It is possible that further on, there will be nods the 80s and the 90s, moving forward while leaning on a changing and altered heritage."

In the recent years, we have witnessed a return of items from the 50s and 60s as well as interior features, in a quasi-nostalgic longing.

Three seater sofa, armchairs, coffee table, foot rest stool and wall unit from the 50s, Shomrat-Hazorea. Photo courtesy of Shomrat-Hazorea.

Clockwise: Television wall unit from the 70s, Shomrat-Hazorea. Photo courtesy of Shomrat-Hazorea; A stylish armchair, designed by Kibbutz Hazorea at the 50s; A Yugoslavian dining chair from the 60s; American Accordion lamp from the 60s. Last three are Vintage items restored by "Fibers Studio," used in current Israeli Interior design. Photography: Amir Lahav

The Israeli design scene has developed rapidly, just as the country has developed in all areas, and has now achieved a maturity that proudly taps on the doors of other countries. Israeli designers are warmly adopted by international design companies, design projects from Israel star in well-known and respected magazines and internet sites, and the profession is an inseparable part of the free professions reaching the entire country - center to periphery. It is often defined by the designers themselves as "the best profession in the world."

Check your taste

If you feel connected to:

...you like nostalgia 16

...you have a classy existence 72

...you appreciate beauty and are minimalistic 90

...you are grounded and up-to-date 154

... you are floating in space 174

Nostalgic Grandma Chic
Continuing the Heritage

Mixing together: Armchairs from the flea market, wooden tables with carved legs, an old radio, grinder, scales, typewriter, patterned tiles, Moreno glass light fixtures, wooden Danish furniture, rounded angles, wooden shutters, laced glass, Capitonnage sofas, retro wallpaper, doors and windows from old houses, family photos in sepia (old brown, as from the past) or yellowing black-and-white.

Dining area surrounded by large floral wallpaper, with a vintage table and old
chairs purchased from a vintage dealer and covered with colorful graphic fabric.
Interior Design: Tal Meidan, Studio Diratili. Photography by Orit Arnon.

Classic items add charm and character to any space, whether it's retro or rustic, modern or contemporary.

Sitting corner of the living room with an old refurbished armchair and a lamp from a second-hand shop.
Interior Design: Merav Zohar.
Photography by Shiran Carmel.

Strainers as part of the rustic kitchen, were found at the Jaffa flea market and placed over the oven.
Interior Design and Home styling: Liron Otmazgin, Studio Adida. Photography by Shai Epstein.

Grandma rules this style, and not because of archaic or aging design but rather a combination of new and old. The family carries an important value to Israelis, so that items from the home of one's grandmother, mother or aunt have high sentimental value. Life in the kibbutz (a type of settlement which is unique to Israel) in the first years of the state, and the love for hosting and sharing increased the amount of typical furniture items, bequeathing them to Israeli design as they find their way into contemporary homes. Old furniture emotionally charged will not be easily handed away, even if it has had its time and can no longer be used. If it passes from generation to generation, it will blend into the new home design of the children or grandchildren or the nearby neighbor who is just renovating his apartment, no matter what style of design they had chosen. A warm and nostalgic corner with that item will always blend in with a cool modern home (to warm up the atmosphere), Scandinavian or Mediterranean. It is still a highly significant family item, in addition to its saving money and thereby rendering superfluous the buying of new furniture.

Classic items such as teak wood dressers, old globes and out-dated typewriters transcend time and their display adds charm and character to any space, whether it is retro or rustic, modern or contemporary. Combining a single item or several of such should be carried away sensitively to avoid going overboard, while also keeping the item from getting lost.

Sources for finding such items are the flea markets, inheritance from grandmother and aunts, vintage shops that import items from abroad and collect furniture from old houses, and – of course – imitations of old furniture. If a house is emptied and has old components left, the antique dealers arrive, dismantle and keep whatever they consider desired on the market. And if, heavens forbid, the furniture finds itself on the street, it will surely be picked up after 2-3 minutes to the warm embrace of a passerby who will find a way to paint, smooth and alter parts of it, to make it suitable for his or her home, or to the home of others for a symbolic, or larger, sum. Yes, the flea business flourishes, and whoever has a collection of dishes or a fine item can open a business or a virtual shop, participate in fairs and sell their love-ware. The good news is that there are buyers. Apparently in order to create the heart-warming grandma chic look.

A designer's apartment where all of her dreams have come true. New blue kitchen cupboards made of simple Formica have been upgraded by new brass handles. The dining area hosts a second-hand dining table from the flea market with vintage chairs. A joyful floral retro-style wallpaper nods to the 60s and 70s, and the pattern is broken by an enormous brass-framed mirror. Vintage lighting fixtures and eclectic ornamental objects create a rich concept and design.
Interior Design: Tal Meidan, Studio Diratili.
Photography by Orit Arnon.

A bathroom in light colors providing a clean, fresh, minimalist ambiance. The sloped wooden ceiling is painted white, the light floor tiles are by Patricia Urquiola, and the vintage-styled wooden dresser was planned with a shelf for a mirror and ornamentation.
Interior Design: Perri Interior Design.
Photography by Aviad Bar-Ness.

Home dressing that expresses appreciation of design and items of the past and love for color that imbues joy and lightness in the space. Furniture that had been stored for years was combined with furniture items bought at the markets, and wallpapers delineating various functions reinforce the colorfulness.
Home Styling: Victoria Delgo.
Photography by Maor Moyal.

A tower apartment where the design was influenced by the nature of its owner, with old armchairs, an old dining room table from her family's heritage matched with chairs of the same style, and bright young wallpaper compensating for the old look created.
Interior Design: Tal Meidan and Anat Steg on behalf of Studio Diratili.
Photography by Orit Arnon.

In order to create a place of her own inspired by a home she loved, with a calm and pleasing way of life, the designer and design writer created her home with the feelings of belonging, closeness, love and - in particular - the memories connected to her grandmother. Deep colors, grandmother's vintage dishes and furniture living in harmony with contemporary lines, together creating a home with a unique character.

Interior Design and Home Styling: Oran Farbman.
Photography by Shiran Carmel.

A warm, comfortable and pleasant penthouse sets the stage for vintage objects from all over the world. To extend the living room wall, the gypsum wall is inlaid with a "decobrick" mashrabiya, decorating the home entrance like a jewel, while enabling a glimpse to the living room. The aqua color is repeated in the kitchen carpentry behind it.
Interior Design: Yael Engel-Benno.
Photography by Yifat Yogev.

An apartment from the 40s in Haifa, in which the original red bricked walls became a part of the design. The emphasis on the apartment's history is also expressed with old items and in an old style combined with new and contemporary elements and bold colors.
Interior Design: Dana Broza, DANKA design. Photography by Itay Benit.

25

An apartment in an International Style preserved building, in the heart of Tel Aviv. The city itself was an inspiration for the design characterized by eclecticism and exploding colors, while maintaining and reconstructing the ornamental tiles and the original wooden windows. The home comprises decorative elements and Art Deco lighting fixtures alongside contemporary industrial elements.

Architecture and Interior Design: Barak Faust and Arnon Eshed.
Photography by Gidon Levin, 181 Degrees.

Sources for finding such items are the flea markets, inheritance from grandmother, aunts and vintage shops.

A vintage style entryway chest of drawers for keys and objects. At the back of the chest the wall was taken down, and in its place there is an expansive kitchen island.
Interior Design: Limor Oren. Photography by Orit Arnon.

> Combining a single item or several should be carried away sensitively to avoid going overboard.

A breathtaking view framed by old shutters, bought second-hand. Moderate colorfulness, green indoors and out, and natural materials such as wood, rope and linen blend with shelves, a macramé curtain and furniture of sentimental value. Together with the lighting fixtures, metal birds, ornamental sanitary devices and an abundance of plants, a warm home has been created, unique and inviting.
Design and Home Styling: Michal Silberstein.
Photography by Dalia Shahar.

28

An apartment that reflects the character of its inhabitants, the designer and photographer, through the use of restored vintage pieces that were inherited, pieces from the flea market and collected from the street. Textiles, wood and plants create a warm and inviting atmosphere.

In the kitchen, pots and pans hang from a ceiling rack. On the shelves are spices, vegetables, jars with nuts and beans in order to save space in the cabinets.

The dining area is a natural extension of the kitchen. A dining room table and cupboard inherited from family were personally reworked. The vintage shelves, filled with objects in day to day use, add character to the space, serving as an additional space for storing items.

Interior Design: Vered Fichmann.
Photography by Moran Mayan.

Home Styling: Victoria Delgo.
Photography by Maor Moyal.

Interior Design and Home Styling:
Oran Farbman.
Photography by Shiran Carmel.

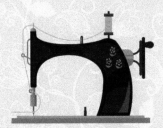

3 PLACES
to Acquire Local Grandma Chic:

1   The Flea Market in Tel-Aviv-Jaffa is the most popular domain in Israel to search for antiques and nostalgic items. This domain is located between Amiad, Olei Hagardom, Yehuda Margoza and Beit Eshel Streets in Jaffa. Veteran shops offer old ware from Israel and abroad. Private peddlers have stands and stalls located during the day in the central market domain, where they await a passersby, reminiscing about the old times and haggling over prices. Over the last few years, following the massive renovation activity of the Tel-Aviv-Jaffa Municipality, new chic shops have opened as well as galleries and artists' studios. The area is flourishing, abundant with restaurants and cafes, even achieving the title of "One of the fifty coolest neighborhoods in the world" by the London-based Time Out magazine.

2   The Haifa Flea Market is the little northern brother of the Jaffa one, which has become commercialized. The Haifa market is located on Kibbutz Galuyot and Wadi Salib Streets, including the alleys between them, and it maintains its nostalgic authenticity since its days as the back yard of the bustling commercial area there over a hundred years ago. Its merchants are second and third generation immigrants to the country, having repopulated the market in the 50s after the State was founded.

3   The magic of private collections has yielded private enterprises of vintage and antique lovers, who have opened fairs and small but exciting shops in their homes or as transient virtual shops selling dishes, items, lighting fixtures and furniture to anyone interested in

Modern Warmth
A warm touch to a cool-ish atmosphere

Mixing together: Hard-edge carpentry devoid of decorations, clean-lined lighting fixtures, integral handles, aluminum, stainless steel, dominant use of wood, shades of white, black, gray, and smoky colors with textiles of the same color scale.

Interior Design: Sivan Itzhaki.
Photography by Elad Gonen. (More on page 46)

The main factor is wood and its shades, whose presence cannot be ignored, especially by its use in the carpentry. Textiles are another central hero of warming up the atmosphere.

Interior Design: Racheli Ben Avi.
Photography by Oded Smadar.
(More on page 44)

Atmosphere of freedom in the bedroom, combining natural materials such as wood, leather and bamboo with custom made cushions.
Interior Design: Yehudit Goldfarb and Natalie Gedalia, Studio YGNG.
Photography by Hila Ido.

I f we try to generalize which of the well-defined styles of design (not the ones found in the book) are most beloved by Israelis, it is likely that the modern line will get most votes. Warm Modern is considered young and updated, and whoever adopts it advocates the slogan "The world belongs to the young" or at least to those young at heart.

In Israel, style has its own interpretations, and the one most prevalent, rendering uniqueness to the style we are dealing with here, is the phenomenon of warming up the atmosphere. Since this style is considered cold, expensive and alienated - often too catalogue-oriented for living space, using straight lines and materials classified as cold such as concrete and stone - the characteristic Israeli translation is the warm modern. Although this may seem to be an oxymoron, there are quite a few apartments elegantly stylized by clean-lined carpentry, non-decorative elements, monochromatic hues, and straight line furniture - to which are added warming factors, as befits a Mediterranean climate residence and rendering the appearance, pleasant and inviting. A quasi-minimalistic yet warm esthetics.

The main factor is wood and its shades, whose presence cannot be ignored, especially by its use in the carpentry. Textiles are another central hero of warming up the atmosphere. A leather armchair, usually suited to modern design, is combined with a throw blanket or cloth cushions of relaxed tones, nearly monochromatic. Carpets can change the atmosphere in a quick spread, since this mass of textile imbues a warm feeling in any modern design. To these are added plants, wall paint in smoked colors of gray, brown, blue or green, and if stone or concrete are used - they are accentuated through the effect of wall color, wall covering, and tiles that are decorated or have embossed texture. If the room has also a typical Grandma Chic item that seemingly threatens to shift to another style, its role is mainly to spice up the space with a warm touch, leaving it faithful to the Modern Warmth style.

The living room concept is elegant, homey, modern and colorful with unique carpentry furniture that expands the kitchen. A laminated parquet floor in a warm walnut hue, furniture, carpet and cushions form a clean colorful line, and accented with meticulously elegant brass lighting.
Interior Design: Tammy Eckhaus. Photography by Omri Amsalem.

> Carpets can change the atmosphere in a quick spread, since this mass of textile imbues a warm feeling in any modern design.

Thanks to the tree growing outside of the apartment, the living room was situated facing it and the opening was broadened to its maximum. An Ikea dresser was upgraded with an oak surface, and the smoked oak parquet, blue hues, textiles and a nostalgic rocking horse from the owner's childhood contribute to the quiet look.
Interior Design: Dana Broza, DANKA design.
Photography by Yoav Peled / Peled Studios.

A light, flowing and well-illuminated space where the prevailing white of walls and kitchen create well-illuminated design. To avoid sterility, a beige stone floor was chosen combined with solid wood, a cable carpet and upholstery introducing warmth and a homey feeling. The lighting fixtures intensify the effect in the evening.
Architecture: Ilanit Argaman. Photography by Lior Teitler.

A living room for entertaining and family relaxation in front of the TV, designed with warmth and harmony, and connecting to the garden. Natural materials of stone, wood and concrete contrast with a clean white wall and shiny nickel, as well as collected items harking to personal experiences.
Interior Design: Ira Sarig.
Photography by Galit Deutsch.

Straight lines and quiet light colors combined with natural materials such as metal, wood, stone and textile items, creating a warm, pleasant atmosphere and quiet design.
Interior Design: Chen Baron. Photography by Oded Smadar.

An urban chic in a design that looks effortless, with a young design alongside a reserved look. Various hues of gray are the prevailing color in the home, combined with wood, and pictures that provide touches of color.
Interior Design: Racheli Ben Avi. Photography by Oded Smadar.

A mini penthouse in modern design with rustic touches of textile and carpentry. A geometric carpet is spread on the oak-wood parquet with a uniquely designed buffet. The wall has Arava plaster.

Interior Design: Sivan Itzhaki. Photography by Elad Gonen.

An apartment in a new tower overlooking an urban view that spreads out to the sea and penetrates the public space, emphasizing the ambiance of a warm urban loft. The kitchen wall is covered with natural pine boards, unifying and enlarging the kitchen area and the dining room opens to the living-room. The kitchen work is conducted on a black marble counter overlooking the view.

Interior Design: Ifat Huber.
Photography by Yoav Peled / Peled Studios.

An impressive while reserved private home in the Jerusalem Ein Kerem quarter, with a warm and timeless modern design line, reflecting the religious family living there. The living room furniture is leather, and holy books decorate the wooden and iron shelves. As behooves a Haredi household, in place of a television there is a screen of changing pictures.

Interior Design and architecture: Orit Cohavi.
Photography by Shai Epstein.

An entertaining area composed of monotone colors, expressed in the gray tiling of the living room and the wooden parquet in the kitchen. The colors, textures and materials help reduce the size and create a warm homey ambiance, with a fireplace located at the center of the staircase and a CNC-cut screen beside it.
Interior Design: Nitzan Horovitz. Photography by Oded Smadar.

Green armchairs and two wooden bookcases designed as an undulating snake in hues of wood and black create a symmetry between the fireplace and the windows, granting the family a quiet haven. A lighting bar perpetuates the soft atmosphere, emphasizing design elements.

Architecture and Interior Design: Yaara Krakover.
Photography by Elad Gonen.

A young modern design concept of a Tel Aviv bachelor apartment in gray hues with touches of wood and yellow. The open staircase and the glass railing keep the space light.
Architecture and Interior Design: Yaara Krakover. Photography by Elad Gonen.

3 FACTORS
Upgrading the Modern Style to Modern Warmth:

ART

Beyond the cultural value of art in one's home, it has the additional value of warming up the atmosphere. It introduces interest by virtue of its being, and it captures one's eye, especially if it is dominant in size and colors.

WOOD

When it is colored black, it is industrial. When it is colored white it imbues a cold charm. And when it is natural, brown hues, it is the epitome of nature, the immediate comforter and the ultimate warmth-provider.

TEXTILE

Whether it is a carpet spread out in the living room, curtains decorating the windows, or multiple cushions on the sofa - there is nothing like textile to soften a cool atmosphere, even if the carpet is colorless, the cushions are neutral, and the curtains are pure as snow. The rich texture is the true tie-breaker.

Polite Urbanity
Industrial with Class

Mixing together: Concrete, aluminum or black iron profiles, aluminum shutters, gray or white furniture, iron net, iron elements, brushed steel, white and black bathroom equipment, clean carpentry, combination of wood and metal, exposed infrastructures.

Interior Design: Shlomit Gliks.
Photography by Oded Smadar.
(More on page 71)

53

The Polite Urbanity style dictates industrial elements that are contemporary and minimalist - but not rough and crude with a raw industrial feeling.

Small kitchen in black and white concept with natural materials of wood, concrete, iron and brass. To create a sense of space and illusion of size, the kitchen structure was stretched, and continuous lines were emphasized, horizontal and vertical.
Interior Design: Sarit Ziv Alon. Photography by Itay Benit.

*Interior Design: Yehudit Goldfarb
and Natalie Gedalia, Studio YGNG.
Photography by Hila Ido.*

We have mentioned that Israelis in general love the modern style, and here is an additional translation into modernity, tugging in the industrial direction, yet not tugging all the way - rather, maintaining elegance and even warmth. The dominant colors and materials are black iron, aluminum, concrete and an array of grays. The very popular combination of wood and metal, imbues a touch of warm and delicate industrialism. Color emphasis maintains outdoor colors of the sky and earth, to which are added smooth, thin furniture legs, thin black lamp cables, and even the warm carpet or parquet floor that push aside the metallic and cool sensations emanating from this style, leaving them on a low burner or at least not dominant.

As opposed to the Modern Warmth style, the Polite Urbanity style dictates industrial elements that are contemporary and minimalist - but not rough and crude with a raw industrial feeling. Rather, these elements are delicate, thin and soft, as if they were devised and suited visually to a home space. The ceiling, beam or air conditioning duct, for instance, may be visible, but with a clean look, elegant and state-of-the-art - not too jungle-like or crude.

The urban style according to its official definition refers to planning and design of areas and public buildings, and it is therefore characterized by durable and industrial materials, suitable for the multitudes and outdoor conditions. Take street elements, mix them with minimalism, and place them together in a modern room of a home. What did you get? Contrast of soft along hard and modern industrial that gives the home a comfortable and inviting feeling. Or in other words: polite and delicate urbanity.

A penthouse emphasizing the building's surroundings and urban life where the view impacts on the interior, the boundaries between them are blurred, and the choice of materials and colors is identical. The presence of nature creates a feeling of vitality and freshness of the materials.

Interior Design: Aviram-Kushmirski Studio, Oshri Aviram and Dana Kushmirski. Photography by Oded Smadar.

Natural materials such as iron, stone and wood in their primary form appear in a transitional space from the public area to the personal one. A metal cupboard hides the washing and drying machines, and the remaining elements are the owner's collections of items.
Interior Design: Ira Sarig. Photography by Galit Deutsch.

Multiple exits to the yard and an upper window lightening the concrete mass in the central space, enabling introduction of daylight and the color of the sky. Iron beams supporting the roof continue out as a pergola with intertwined iron. The furniture and carpentry were chosen as raw yet precise solutions, rough while not clumsy. The house exterior combines bare concrete-boards and plaster. The floor is smoothed and polished concrete. The bookcase is made of unpainted iron and the kitchen from brushed raw wood.

Architecture and Interior Design: Jacobs - Yaniv Architects.
Photography by Amit Geron.

A warm inviting living room looking out at the owner's orchards. The carpet and coordinated cushions create a strong presence on the background of monochrome walls and furniture.
Interior Design: Carmit Gat.
Photography by Itay Benit.

A central multi-purpose space, serving in the evening for the family to convene, while during the day glass screens enable its closing into an office. The bookcase is covered with wenge wood veneer, and the mobile glass screens have black aluminum profiles. The colorfulness imbues a sense of vitality and joy.
Interior Design: Yifat Moshkovitz. Photography by Elad Gonen.

A modern open home, where the view and the garden are inseparable from the interior. Contemporary materials such as gray stone in the wall and dark basalt stones outside are joined by natural materials of real wooden parquet, iron and stone. The staircase serves as a kitchen pantry.
Architecture: Sharon Weiser. Interior design: Hadas Friedler and Osnat Spivak Shimony, Studio Spivak Friedler.
Photography by Itay Benit.

A compact apartment combining a wooden floor and a concrete ceiling, a wooden veneer and iron, introducing an urban dimension corresponding with the view outdoors. The kitchen cupboards and the white tiles create a sense of depth and reflection through various degrees of polish, thereby visually expanding the space. An iron construction with plants imbues a feeling of urban nature inside the home.
Interior Design: Nitzan Horovitz. Photography by Oded Smadar.

A penthouse apartment in black, white and touches of color. A gray sofa, black velvet armchair, and coffee tables in hues of black and gray are delineated in the living room by a modern gray carpet. The dramatic TV chest somewhat conceals the TV, and the black mass at the white wall creates depth. Touches of yellow with light steps in blue, introduce lightness, color and character to the space.
Interior Design: Maya Sheinberger. Photography by Itay Benit.

Contrary to the common notion that small spaces require light colors, the main furniture item chosen to extend the length of the apartment is in black wood veneer, creating a black-tie festive atmosphere. It conceals a wine bar, audio system, air-conditioning system, open shelving of books and ornamental objects, and closed compartments for storage. At its home entry side, there is a "Pole Dancer" storage for coats, keys and other items.

Architecture: Rony Avitzour and Ofer Rossmann, XS Studio for Compact Design. Project Architect: Avital Broide. Photography by Amit Gosher.

The kitchen is the beating heart of the family space due to its location and special hue, balanced by carpentry details of wood veneer and a bookcase of wood and iron. The kitchen wall is covered with blocks.
Interior Design: Roni Keren.
Photography by Yoav Gurin.

A kitchen in straight and elegant lines, with a wall surrounding the tall cupboards in an identical hue creating a dark block in the space, thereby intensifying the sharpness and elegance of the cupboards, and defining the kitchen area. The clean lines are interrupted by the asymmetrical location of the lighting fixtures with a loose and dangling cord. Concrete-like ceramic tiles serve as a live and non-unified base for the hard-edge furniture above it.
Interior Design: Carmit Gat.
Photography by Itay Benit.

The design of a young couple's apartment was inspired by their honeymoon in the Caribbean Islands. A palette of warm natural colors and natural materials create a pleasant caressing ambiance, reminiscent of enjoyable days in Africa.

Interior Design: Yehudit Goldfarb and Natalie Gedalia, Studio YGNG. Photography by Hila Ido.

A clean line of black and white hues in the spacious living-room, with authentic items such as drums that serve as tables, and a white sofa for reclining. The dark iron hardware on the large iron bookcase and the windows give the stylistic tone. *Architecture and Interior Design: Sara and Nirit Frenkel. Photography by Itay Benit.*

68

The concept of industrial minimalism has led to the use of concrete, iron and wood repeated in furniture items and constructive elements of a home maintaining an open airy space. The kitchen is delineated by the gallery's floor above it with iron beams, and surrounded by a concrete beam defining its boundaries. An iron bookcase combined with wood separates the entrance and the living-room. A steel staircase with a grid iron railing leads to a floor of warm rooms with a sense of an industrial loft, including pictures that suit the nature of the family.

Interior Design: Shir Shtaigman. Architecture: Zarta Studio. Photography by Itay Benit.

Design balancing mass and lightness, precision and roughness, used and new, while maintaining a clean design style expressed by simplicity. An L-shaped kitchen embraces an island and a dining table to maintain the family togetherness. The kitchen style is rough with a coal-black front and a Caesarstone counter in very dark gray. The mass is lightened by black brass handles. The island is coal-black and over it a white Caesarstone surface, which maintains visual cleanness. Adjacent to the tables are light and natural iconic chairs and above them lighting fixtures with brass finishing.

Interior Design: Roni Bartal Shalem.
Photography by Itay Benit.

A bachelor's apartment in the crowded Tel Aviv urban view, with a style preserving the sense of raw and kicking, while also creating an inviting, warm and intimate place. On one hand, preserving and exposing concrete beams and columns, and the use of architectural concrete slabs, while on the other – fishbone-laid parquet, warm red dismantled bricks, a light sofa and soft textiles. Touches of yellow, copper and black add to the vibrant and saucy atmosphere.

Interior Design: Shlomit Gliks. Photography by Oded Smadar.

HOW WILL YOU KNOW
if Your Home is Urban but Polite?

If the home contains black color, and a lot of it, or as a dominant element in the space, for instance the window profiles, the kitchen color, carpentry or walls, then you are surely inside. But wait a moment. Not only that will determine the style. To create the politeness of the urbanity, there is a softening step lacking that comes in the form of grids; furniture with a modern-industrial look and thin legs, a colorful or full carpet, dressers or wooden elements, a textured or colorful wall, and cushions and small touches of a warm color. Imagine the hard core of the industrial style, and now tone it down and turn it into homey and softened style.

Reserved Luxury
Prestige between the Walls

Mixing together: Velvet cloth, shiny upholstery, leather, rich textile, touches of metallic or gold, dark colors, marble, shine, carpentry or carpentry covering of whole walls, items of super designers, a lowered ceiling with recessed lighting

A relaxed space for the couple who work at various hours of the day, with a contrast between cold modern materials conveying luxury, such as concrete and nickel versus leather, velvet, chiffon and ornamental items in rose gold. The latter imbue warmth and soften the space, creating a connection between masculine and feminine, and between night and day.
Interior Design: Elephant Design. Photography by Lior Teitler.

The furniture as well as the textiles will always look comfortable, rich and superb, as if they were picked out of a catalogue or straight from a luxury hotel.

Interior Design: Dalit Vengrovsky.
Photography by Elad Gonen.
(more on page 86)

Interior Design: Aviram-Kushmirski Studio,
Oshri Aviram and Dana Kushmirski.
Photography by Oded Smadar.
(more on page 79)

Always looking modern and too expensive to obtain - that is the modern luxury style full of modern chic. This style gives the feeling that every corner is treated to the smallest detail, and no wall is orphaned. The carpentry extends over entire walls, to their precise measurements. They may have secret doors, leading to back spaces not noted at first. The kitchen and bathroom tiles are superb, from marble, concrete or their artificial versions, and also extend massively over entire walls and surfaces, often encompassing a space from floor to ceiling. The ceiling is lowered by rational treatment, and contains recessed or concealed lighting fixtures. The furniture as well as the textiles will always look comfortable, rich and superb, as if they were picked out of a catalogue or straight from a luxury hotel.

The lighting fixtures are made by the best super designers or at least highly branded. The styling items imbue this as well, so that if they are not produced by a prestigious shop, at least they shine with gold touches as befits high class prestige. The colors characterizing the style are usually dark, such as black, gray or blue, but even white and various shades of beige can give the same look, provided that the spaces are equipped with the factors mentioned above. The dark furniture, such as a black metallic coffee table, has a gold item added to it, maintaining a metallic appearance and granting a touch of warmth and color, while sofas, armchairs and other velvet elements caress the space.

These colors convey maturity, seriousness and elegance, stating that prudent and careful people live here, who never express liveliness or playfulness - which would be reflected in more cheerful colors. The style is very clean while refraining from being minimalist, and it broadcasts a type of seriousness. The luxury style pays attention to details and finishes, and the materials are at the high end of the price range, as expressed in their appearance as well.

An extensive sleeping suite of two combined rooms, designed in dark hues of dark brown, mocha, cream and natural oak wood. The design gives the feeling of refined elegance and an aroma of luxury with an elongated, upholstered bed with extra space, for whatever comes to mind. The textiles are rich with details, a floating ceiling conceals the lighting and curtains, and a chocolate-hue oak bookcase unit seems to burst through the ceiling. The airy design allows the entrance of light from the walk-in closet behind it.

Interior Design: Isabelle Ofra Ichai.
Photography by Elad Gonen.

Raw materials received personality, movement and life in a performance of unconventional connections between form, materials, textures, objects and art. The kitchen island is oval and above it is an oval lighting fixture. Rounded screens of iron and glass are covered by a mirror. The designing of shaped textures in the coverings, elements and furniture are all intensified by light and shadow.

Interior Design: Aviram-Kushmirski Studio, Oshri Aviram and Dana Kushmirski.
Photography by Oded Smadar.

The style is very clean while refraining from being minimalist, and it broadcasts a type of seriousness. The luxury style pays attention to details and finishes, and the materials are at the high end of the price range, as expressed in their appearance as well.

Similarly to nature, composed of layers, the natural materials were granted new expression and context by the meeting of materials in a masterpiece of layers. The carpentry casing of wooden bars conceals storage units and doors, and thin shelves of punctured brass texture create a floating bookcase.

Interior Design: Aviram-Kushmirski Studio, Oshri Aviram and Dana Kushmirski. Photography by Oded Smadar.

A penthouse in the port town of Ashdod, with an abundance of natural light emphasizing reserved colorfulness. The sea is echoed in blue covered walls and textiles in the dining area. An iron bookcase, open at both ends, separates it from the hall and extends the view towards the outdoors. Original art items are spread around the home.

Architecture: Oshir Asaban. Photography by Oded Smadar.

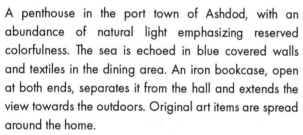

To create a pleasant, calm and balanced environment in a garden apartment, a neutral monochromatic color scheme was chosen with light touches of color on the furniture and items. The style shifts between modern and classic, and between elegant and rough with natural materials such as wood, stone and various types of metal.
Interior Design: Chen Baron. Photography by Oded Smadar.

A central space on the 22nd floor of a Tel Aviv tower
was designed open to the sea. The balcony contains sofas of Israeli design.
Architecture: Oshir Asaban.
Photography by Gidon Levin, 181 degrees.

81

A private home in Neo-Classic rustic style, warm and homey, contains a round staircase with an artist-created iron railing. The dining area wall cover replicates dismantled bricks. The fireplace and natural parquet floor lend warmth to the space. The windows are wooden in their inner side, and the lowered ceiling incorporates the air-conditioning and lighting fixtures.

Architecture and Interior Design: Moshik Hadida.
Photography by Oded Smadar.

A penthouse with a prestigious, modern and dramatic look, combining straight clean lines, bold colors and fabric of leather, velvet and wool. The blue furniture corresponds with the outdoor pool, and the floor marble tiles are extra-large. *Interior Design: Inbal Berkovich. Photography by Elad Gonen.*

A living room with a luxurious and elegant look, in which a cupboard of light birch wood veneer serves as a central axis in the space, and a frame of brass-painted tin grants it luxury and power. A rich textile of net curtains with underlining, a prestigious carpet in hues of brown-gray, a leather couch, velvet-covered armchairs, iron tables combined with glass in a metal look and the gray color prevailing on the marble-like floor, all create calm and warmth.

Interior Design: Dalit Vengrovsky. Photography by Elad Gonen.

A Tel Aviv apartment with artistic chic inspired by the Tel Aviv nightlife and the world of New York lofts. Metal finishing materials combined with exposure of the old building's structural treasures, creating masculine industrial architecture, while the furniture and home dressing introduce softness and eclecticism of an artistic loft.
Architecture: Yaron Eldad. Interior Design: Yehudit Goldfarb and Natalie Gedalia, Studio YGNG.
Photography by Omri Amsalem.

A long narrow apartment in which the axis is accentuated, from the entrance to the balcony by extended carpentry with stations for storage of clothes and shoes at the entrance. Kitchen utensils face the kitchen, serving dishes and concealed bar face the dining area, and video/audio products face the living room. The soothing colors hark to the mountainous hues outdoors, and the lighting fixtures, both overt and concealed, emphasize each function.
Architecture and Interior Design: Adi Aronov. Photography by Amit Gosher.

Graphic elements create a harmonious play of shapes and lines in a minimalistic, clean and sophisticated space. Monochromatic hues combined with touches of color and ornamental objects to create a pleasant and warm atmosphere.
Interior Design: Dalit Vengrovsky.
Photography by Elad Gonen.

Dark and rich colors, creating a European atmosphere, wintry, familial and embracing in a family penthouse. The living room contains a green bookcase, above it art works from the owners' collection, and the sitting area has a pleasant pampering sofa in turquoise and a green armchair with brass legs, making it inviting to sit and read.
Interior Design: Alla Tzecher.
Photography by Itay Benit.

WAYS TO HELP TURN THE STYLE
of Any Home into a Luxurious One:

Luxury is connected to that time of the year when we pamper ourselves in a hotel; put our head on a fluffy pillow, get off the bed onto a soft carpet and walk over to a boiling bath with plenty of running water and scented soap from the plains of Provence. In order to introduce those sensations into our home, at least partially and not to let the vacation end, we can sprinkle in a bit of the luxury - even if we do not have chocolate and newspapers on our bedspread every day.

Let us begin with the entrance to the home, which should be as impressive as the entrance to a well-designed hotel lobby, with a console table upon which we have a lamp and a vase with fresh flowers. We will choose impressive curtains for the living room and add lighting for ambience either there or in the attached kitchen. We will make certain that the temperature is pleasant, neither too hot nor too cold, and we will devote attention to one of the most neglected rooms in the house - the bedroom. A high quality mattress and linen, headboard, curtains, a throw rug beside the bed, a vanity dressing table and closet, should blend in terms of their design language or colors. We'll have a glass shower in the bedroom, or at least a pretty and designed shower curtain, a large mirror, folded or rolled up towels, soaps and decorative candles. The objective is to live at home in hotel style.

Calculated Graphic Composition

Two Dimensional Becomes Three Dimensional

Mixing together: White mass, black and gray elements, clear and accentuated geometrical shapes, colored blocks or a light touch of blue, pink, green colors and wood, thin black aluminum and black grout between the tiles

Interior Design: Perri Interior Design.
Photography by Gidon Levin, 181 degrees.
(More on page 99)

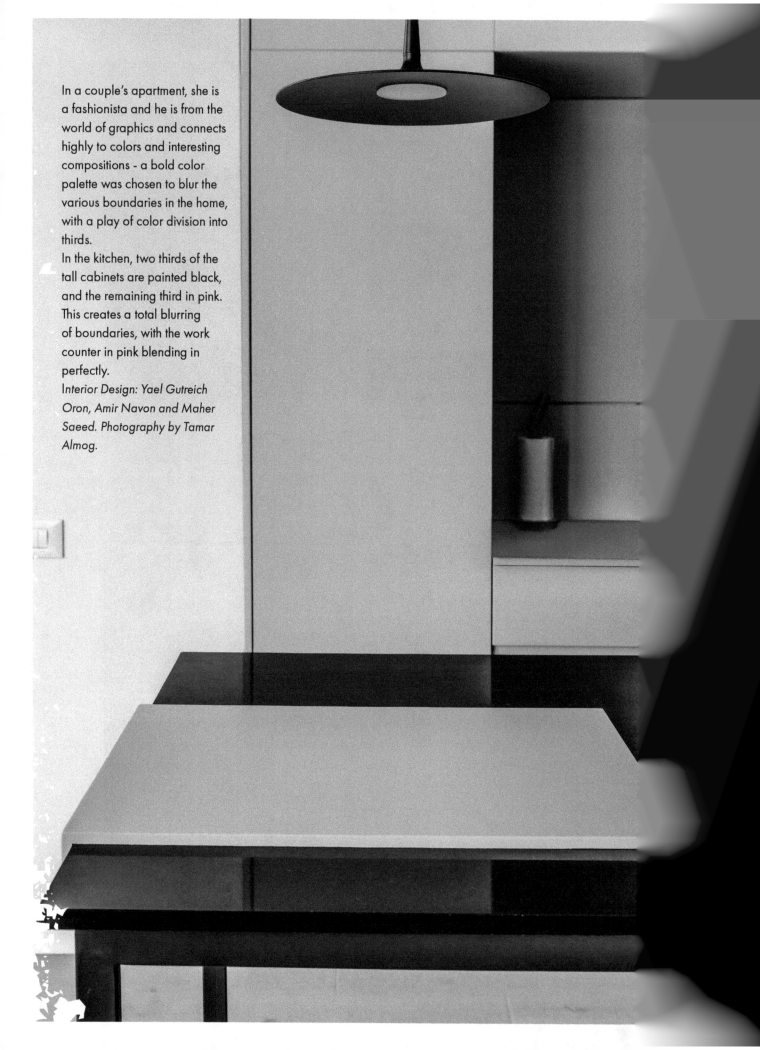

In a couple's apartment, she is a fashionista and he is from the world of graphics and connects highly to colors and interesting compositions - a bold color palette was chosen to blur the various boundaries in the home, with a play of color division into thirds.

In the kitchen, two thirds of the tall cabinets are painted black, and the remaining third in pink. This creates a total blurring of boundaries, with the work counter in pink blending in perfectly.

Interior Design: Yael Gutreich Oron, Amir Navon and Maher Saeed. Photography by Tamar Almog.

Imagine a large white blank sheet of paper, upon which lines and dots begin to appear as well as geometric shapes such as rectangles, squares, ellipses, circles, triangles or grids. They are precise, with the black outlines of the marker that draws them, and the paper is left white and airy enough to let us focus on the shapes. This is the Calculated Graphic Composition style, which converts two dimensional into three dimensional in the space.

The design line is largely modern and minimalistic, devoid of ornamentation, abundant in pure white or transparent elements with black frames, or black and gray standing out on a white background. If there are colors, they will remind us of the Nordic style, using blues, pinks, greens or wood - the colors of nature peeking through the windows of Scandinavia or Israel, in our case. Even if other bolder colors are included in this design, they will appear as measured touches complementing the composition and maintaining balance and proportion; for instance as recessed niches that receive a spot of another color.

The design applies familiar geometric shapes, halved or complete, and creates regular and organized structures, often even symmetrical, which the eye identifies as balanced and proportionate blocks. No element of theirs will "get out of the lines" and disrupt the measured composition - neither collages of pictures, nor rich styling or tropical plants. At the very most, there will be items of graphic appearance that fit into the design pattern. Design according to this style is immediately translated in our minds into "right and good design" (although parallel styles are not devoid of that) - due to the sense of balance and serenity that the space evokes, and to the esthetics that we attribute to whatever we view as organized, symmetric, clean and harmonious.

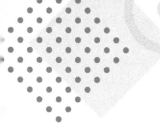

Natural light reflects off the red glass and imbues the bathroom with shades that change throughout the day.
Interior Design: Yael Perry. Photography by Itay Benit.

Carpentry work creates a frame for a picture of the view, combining the bookcase and plants. A black iron showcase continues the design language of frames.
Interior Design: Amir Navon, Maayan Zusman, Ayelet Dar.
Photography by Gidon Levin, 181 degrees.

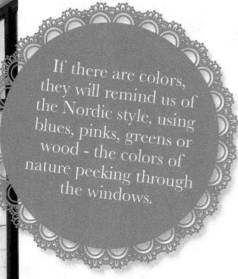

If there are colors, they will remind us of the Nordic style, using blues, pinks, greens or wood - the colors of nature peeking through the windows.

A design based on maximal use of structure geometry, such as window openings, beams and columns, as well as non-trivial connections between spaces through glimpses, views and access. The kitchen space contains an exposed original beam and column, and the cabinet fronts were emphasized by inner frames. The window to the view is framed by carpentry that affords a sitting space.
Interior Design: Amir Navon, Maayan Zusman, Karen Brockman.
Photography by Itay Benit.

A small bedroom in black and white with natural materials such as linen curtains, furniture made of solid wood, and lighting fixtures of brass and metal. To create a sense of height, the black color climbs up to the ceiling.
Interior Design: Sarit Ziv Alon. Photography by Itay Benit.

A kitchen designed lightly and humorously with a composition of colored storage cubes, and walnut wood veneer covering, hanging on the wall covered by a grid of tiles. The kitchen cupboards are painted with two gray hues and have pink button handles that introduce a touch of color to the space.
Interior Design: Perri Interior Design.
Photography by Gidon Levin, 181 degrees.

The headboard of the bed in the bedroom is in saturated blue, and so is part of the closet located precisely behind it. The sides of the wall are in the same color to create a play of depth and dimension as well as boundaries, with the bed and closet swallowed into each other.
Interior Design: Yael Gutreich Oron, Amir Navon and Maher Saeed. Photography by Tamar Almog.

In a ground floor apartment rectangular and elongated, minimally designed, the areas of the kitchen and dining area are defined by blocks of color in the carpentry and the walls. The elongated structure also affected the linear planning of the lighting and placing the parquet flooring lengthwise, from the entrance to the yard.
Interior Design: Carmit Gat.
Photography by Itay Benit.

A Jaffa apartment with sophistication and interesting geometry, providing a hotel daily experience with maximum openness, introduction of natural light, and plenty of space for hosting. The colors create a clean sense of material and colorfulness together with simplicity of design, and the public space contains the kitchen, dining area, sofa, shelves and workstation in the form of rows.
Interior Design: Eitan Cohen, Studio ETN.
Photography by Gidon Levin, 181 degrees.

A bed in the center of the bedroom, open to a shared space and closed by a glass screen with iron divisions in black. The wall closet extends from floor to ceiling, and a black iron beehive contains a collection of robots. An upholstered furniture item serves as the bed's headboard, concealing it from sight and serving as an additional storage space.

A bathroom with a simple yet sophisticated geometric play of black and white tiles. Above them the designated black polyurethane paint for the moist areas adds sparkle to the bathroom. The wall and ceiling are detached in a sophisticated way through an aluminum profile painted black. The shower cubicle reflected in the mirror creates a black bubble for a sense of calm and quiet, and a yellow storage unit lends a humorous and surprising shot of color.

Interior Design: Eitan Cohen, Studio ETN.
Photography by Gidon Levin, 181 degrees.

A young couple's bedroom where an iron and glass screen allows for natural light from the window. The green outdoors environment enters through a natural oak parquet, window carpentry and a color scale of deep green-gray and powder pink for a contemporary look. The accessories complete the concept of an urban jungle, adding to the light and young atmosphere.

Interior Design: Dana Broza, DANKA Design. Photography by Itay Benit.

A bed wall in deep blue, and dark wooden parquet floor, fishbone style, for a warm embracing look. The bed was dressed with textile items of changing textures for a deep yet clean look, and the brass lighting fixtures hang on a black cord over straw footrests that add to the eclecticism.
Interior Design: Carmit Gat.
Photography by Itay Benit.

A bathing space in clean airy lines, intensifying and emphasizing the deep color of the cupboard.
Interior Design: Carmit Gat.
Photography by Itay Benit.

3 INSTAGRAM ACCOUNTS
using a graphic design language

1

deborahmindel

336 posts   1,837 followers   403 following

Deborah Mindel
Photographer & stylist. Blogger
Calligraphy workshops
DM to collaborate
Deborahmindel@gmail.com
deborah-mindel.com

work   moments   shop   HOME   calligraphy   mood boa...   my 50th b...

⊞ POSTS   ⎙ TAGGED

deborahmindel

Deborah Mindel is a window display and commercial positioning designer, who built her home in Eilat and uses it as her studio for workshops or photography and styling for products sent to her. She returns them in the form of a series of photos edited after she has built them into a concept and photo set in her kitchen, pantry, bathroom, bedroom or her private garden.
Photography by Deborah Mindel.

Illustrations   חשיבה - ויז   Quotes   Family   Your words   Portfolio

POSTS   IGTV   TAGGED

2

sapir_benda

Sapir Benda, or in her original name Sapir Ben David, has lived and breathed design since a young age. Alongside design, creativity is what drives her most, and that is why she has been working with paper for several years, and studies graphic design at the Sapir Academic College in Sderot. She enjoys life, travels around the world, getting her inspiration from almost everything. She is addicted to planners, stickers, home design and colors.
Photography by Sapir Ben David.

3

Micush Pr...   Life   Illustration   Collaborat...

POSTS   TAGGED

micushillustration

Michal Marko has an illustration and lifestyle brand that offers notebooks, trays, prints, cards, etc. The collections that she creates are influenced by the romantic feeling of seasonal changes, nature, outdoors. All of the products are decorated with her own original illustrations and prints, characterized by their delicate and nostalgic nature. Micush is currently distributed in several boutiques around the world.
Photography by Aya Wind.

Cozy Home
Warm, Pleasant, Familial

Mixing together: "Fluffy" sofas full of material, a leather sofa preferably wrinkled, seating areas full of cushions, casual style, blankets, curtains, shaggy carpets, plants, colors abundant in textures.

A small apartment, characterized by a richness of colors, materials, textures, prints, textile and plants. It was planned for a bold fashionable owner who is not afraid of unconventional combinations. A sensual maximalist apartment with Parisian chic, all sage green, powder pink and deep blue.
Interior Design: Vered Bonfiglioli.
Photography by Itay Benit.

A design of an apartment with children in a colorful and happy atmosphere inspired by Mexican colors. The apartment combines styles, materials and textures, such as textile, handmade kilim carpets, and art items made in Israel, creating a sense of variety and eclecticism.
Home Styling and Interior Design: Orly Mor.
Photography by Noa Lutski.

Designing of the communal space at home often begins with the sofa. This is the biggest, most massive furniture item among the heavy-weight moveable items populating the living room, and its choice often indicates the stylistic direction preferred by the homeowners. Square, straight and tight is a favorite among the modernists, while soft with wooden legs suits the lovers of the rustic look.

There are, however, middle sofas that suit both or mix with every style. We will see them once with the industrial style, once with the rustic or bohemian, with the Nordic, or the hi-tech. In the cozy home style, the sofas have the same obligatory look - the sofa is casual, slightly wrinkled, looks like someone had just sat on it a moment ago and in a moment he will do so again, only with a plunge. It is deep and invites us to leave the outdoors and stay at home forever; a getaway.

Warm elements such as cushions, blankets, books, lamps, baskets and plants wrap around the sofa, enabling viewers of the living room to imagine how they are drawn into it, sitting or lying on the sofa and using all of the accessories strewn around it. The same goes for sitting in a sitting area or lying on a bed.

There is a sense of coziness, warm and embracing, so that it is almost possible to lay one's hand on the photo and feel how comfortable and inviting it is there. And the conclusion is nearly one: in this house live warm people who are far from minimalism, and do not find the harmony of plants or the play area for children bothersome. If we had to give one tip for this style, we would advise choosing furniture that no one is afraid to use and the guests will feel comfortable sitting on them. If you have chosen a spectacular item for a lot more money than it is worth, then you are in the wrong style. Go to Reserved Luxury.

A home with children that has clean lines and a warm, joyful, fresh and colorful look. The staircase is in mustard yellow, the eclectic living room is full of fabrics and textures, with a cognac-colored leather sofa. The chaise longue was reupholstered in blue velvet and a colorful carpet completes the style. A mask adds a touch of humor.
Interior Design: Dikla Glazer.
Photography by Shiran Carmel.

A family room, broad and full of light, serving as a corner for a reclining chair in front of the TV, a work area for doing homework, and an exit to the garden. An eclectic collection of furniture items, wallpaper, fishbone parquet, carpet, mashrabiya cupboard and accessories create warmth and interest together with a relaxed, timeless family feeling.
Interior Design: Ira Sarig. Photography by Elad Gonen.

A bedroom in black for elegance and drama, joined by items and textiles with character and texture of nature imbuing warmth and balance, such as parquet flooring and a carpet in natural textures, reading lamps for relaxed atmosphere, bedspread, pictures and barn door leading to a bathroom with a similar character.
Interior Design: Osnat Berman.
Photography by Orit Arnon.

A home with dynamics of happiness and discourse through feelings of comfort, warmth and closeness to nature. Bookcase of metal and teak wood, 6 meters high, is seen from all of the sitting areas, connecting between the spaces. Wood, elements of light and plants connect to nature, and fabrics, carpets and art introduce warmth and depth.
Interior Design: Yael Benisti. Photography by Golan Benisti.

A warm, casual look of the family reclining corner in a part of the balcony that was opened up. The corner combines collections and romantic vintage furniture with items and textile in a semi-oriental colorfulness and style.
Home Styling and Photography by Dafna Bareket.

An apartment planned for a light and urban residential-experience of a quasi-loft, soft and homey. Black metal stairs, a cable railing, rough bricks and a natural, fissured oak parquet flooring combined with hues of black-gray, white and vivid blue, adding warmth and a personal touch.

Architecture and Interior Design: Shira Muskal and Hadas Roth, Halel Studio. Photography by Oded Smadar.

The windows of a large, well-illuminated and open space became the central motif of the home's design, around which was built a long bench connecting the living room and the kitchen. On one part it serves as a reading corner, on the other it serves as a seat for the dining table. Light colors contribute to a sense of openness, and the use of wood grants a warm rustic feeling together with the modern style.
Interior Design: Lilach Lempel.
Photography by Dana Stempler Asael.

A living room of relatively narrow dimensions where an abundance of textiles create a sense of depth and a rich look. A long sofa of suede-looking fabric with narrow arms maximizes the seating space, and a cotton carpet creates an illusion of spaciousness. A wealth of plants blends in with a rattan armchair and straw baskets, connecting to the green view outdoors.

Interior Design and Home Styling: Liron Otmazgin, Studio Adida.
Photography by Shai Epstein.

A modern apartment with clean lines, a living room wall in deep dramatic blue, pictures of vibrant presence, and designed lighting fixtures. The comfortable pampering furniture is in hues of stone gray, and the carpet connects the color palette of the entire apartment.
Interior Design: Maayan Manor and Ravit Reznik, Studio Details.
Photography by Shiran Carmel.

A garden duplex for lovers of nature and open space, where modern and functional items combine with furniture and accessories in natural hues. The walls have a botanical-tropical look connecting the outdoors to the indoors, creating a pastoral ambiance.
Interior Design: Shimrit Kaufman, SK Designers.
Photography by Shai Epstein.

A living space where instead of a picture on the wall, there is a collection of pictures on a shelf in an interesting composition. The design harmony is achieved by the orange color in three spots: clementine segments on the shelf, a side dresser, and a book on the table shelf.

Interior Design: Limor Oren. Photography by Orit Arnon.

A home inundated with light creating an Israeli earthy feel, with a soft look in shared family sitting areas, combined with more intimate and quiet areas. In order to create a warm, authentic experience, natural materials such as types of differently processed wood and iron were chosen. Soft sophisticated colors of blue and smoked pink hues along with touches of green bringing nature indoors contrast with black and gold. The rich textile items from a variety of styles and nostalgic objects create a visual richness and a unique atmosphere.

Interior Design and Home Styling: Tamar Meroz, Keren Gross.
Photography by Shiran Carmel.

A bedroom with a relaxed and peaceful chic where a central role is granted to the personally designed textile. *Interior Design: Yehudit Goldfarb and Natalie Gedalia, Studio YGNG. Photography by Hila Ido.*

Natural, light and relaxed materials in a Tel Aviv garden apartment connected to nature and to the sea. Textile breaks the natural hues and introduces vitality of summer and beach further achieved by dismantled lighting fixtures from ships.
Interior Design: Yehudit Goldfarb and Natalie Gedalia, Studio YGNG. Photography by Hila Ido.

Styling and Interior Design: Orly Mor.
Photography by Noa Lutski.

WHICH PLANTS
Suit the Home?

Plants support the Cozy Home Style, and their presence imbues charm on the home and on you.

Pentas, Euphorbia Diamond Frost, Liriope Muscari, and a sprawling Scaevola by the window and on the partially shaded porch.

Green plants, such as Dracaena marginata, Howea Belmoreana (mini palm) and Dracaena Lemon Lime, love a sunny area of the house without a direct sunlight.

Ferns, Chlorophytum and Begonia in moist areas such as the bathroom, but with a window.

Interior Design: Limor Oren.
Photography by Orit Arnon.

131

Wild Wonderland
Happy and Optimistic Colorfulness

Mixing together: Bold colors such as red, green, magenta pink, yellow, orange, white walls, combinations of complex patterns

A joyful and light home, conveying creative freedom and combining art made by the owner. A natural oak parquet floor serves as a frame for rich colorfulness: light blue kitchen, yellow, pink and gray stools, rich textile, pink and yellow lighting fixtures, a bookcase with a green wall and plants. Combinations of black and white balance the general look, creating harmony.

Interior design: Rona Kenan Fish. Photography by Sigal Bar-el.

A 17 sq. meters studio apartment in an attic at the Tel Aviv Levinsky Market, where the designer went wild with warm colors, plants and art. The concept wall, conveying power, struggle and erupting life energy, is painted royal blue as the basis of the art, and complements the color of the orange sofa and the refurbished armchairs.
Home Styling: Shai Eliezer Zvi. Photography by Shiran Carmel.

Interior design: Rona Kenan Fish.
Photography by Sigal Bar-el.
(More on page 133)

Here you will not find soft pastels or any kind of monochrome. This style of happy and optimistic colorfulness mixes color as children love. Imagine a clown, a circus, a birthday party - this is the style that provides a feeling of experiencing and surprises in every corner. The eyes do not rest for a moment and want more and more of the sights. Abundant, spectacular, connecting a full range of colors attractively, harmoniously, with style, bold and daring, happy and granting joy to its residents and viewers. The basis will usually be white, to contain the multitude of colors and give them the appropriate background and the place to stand out. If you wish, wildness of the Mediterranean, but with an optimistic look to the future.

The combinations and quantities depend on the designer and the home-owner, but the colors will always be saturated, bold and accentuated. Lovers of this style will connect to the saying "Why choose one or two colors when you can choose ten?" And make no mistake, if the combination of two or three colors can cause homeowners sleepless nights over how to do it right, then the combination of more colors is a lot more complicated, since it may slide into a mishmash of colors with no order, statement or harmony. Designers who favor this genre measure each hue, checking its suitability to others, and conducting color testing until they reach the right and precise quantity that forms a fresh and exciting esthetics.

A home in a kibbutz, whose owners wished for a joyful design and were not afraid of any color. The living room leaves no one indifferent to its yellow wall and bold colorfulness is balanced out by the quiet green outdoors.
Interior Design: Osi Katz-Dagan. Photography by Tamar Almog.

The basis will usually be white, to contain the multitude of colors and give them the appropriate background and the place to stand out.

A happy, spacious and well-illuminated home in a kibbutz whose colors were dictated by the yellow, pink and light blue ceiling lamps in the dining area. The kitchen is in light turquoise and the dining table has a mix of six different chairs. There is an Ikea sofa in the living room with cushions made of material found in the costume storage of the kibbutz, an armchair upholstered in pink, a colorful carpet, a collection of paintings, and a wall with yellow stripes.

Interior Design: Hadar Aram. Photography by Shiran Carmel.

Coffee-colored walls, chocolate-brown wallpaper and a carpet taken out of storage are the backdrop for the vintage sofa and armchairs in hues that do well for the carpet. Posters from a trip to Cuba were framed, creating an eclectic and personal combination for the owner who likes brown, uniqueness, bold color, and a singular look.
Interior design: Liat Evron. Photography by Itay Benit.

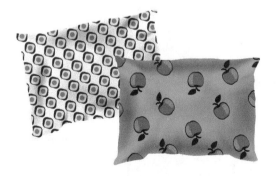

A reclining area with cushions and joyful heart-warming colorfulness. An Orla Kiely leafy wallpaper sets the tone and vintage pictures collected at a second-hand sale abroad complement and reverberate the colorfulness.
Interior design: Liat Evron. Photography by Ilan Nachum.

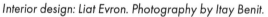

A colorful and happy home, with light modern lines, iron stairs painted white, with oak steps above a carpentry painted green. Through the design, a owners wanted to allude to their being gay, so beyond the warmth, colorfulness and family feeling, there is a picture of Dame Edna, made of 19 thousand colorful toy blocks by artist Eyal Alef Ophir.

Interior design: Liat Evron.

Photography by Shai Epstein.

A vivacious style of the owners, who came to Israel from Hawaii, lent a combination of color, art, yearning, memories and local inspiration to the apartment. The kitchen is in deep blue, the wooden shelves have brass supports combined with built-in lighting fixtures. The blue-gray hand-made Moroccan tiles convey a Mediterranean character. In the dining area, is a wall covering of natural tones. The chairs are upholstered in Catalan fabric that adds touches of yellow.
Interior Design: Shimrit Kaufman, SK Designers. Photography by Avishai Finkelstein.

A kitchen of a family seeking a childhood experience of happiness and informal feeling of non-commitment. Color is introduced in elements such as the light blue kitchen door, chairs, lighting through strainers etc.

Interior Design: Merav Zohar. Photography by Shiran Carmel.

A home in a kibbutz, whose owners wanted a residential, joyful, picturesque and colorful feeling while also balanced. Most of the color is provided by items such as a metal cupboard, kitchen cupboards, door, textile and some furniture bought at second-hand shops, painted and reupholstered.

Interior Design: Merav Zohar. Photography by Shiran Carmel.

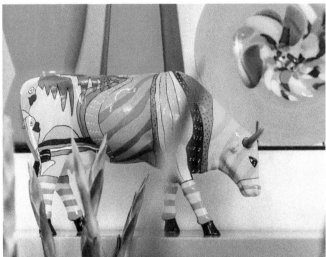

A designer's home, full of light, color and joy, providing her a place for creative thinking, and an artistic and designing expression of spaces, furniture and items suited to a specific space.
Interior Design: Orit Sherman Nahari. Photography by Haim Afriat.

A saturated color palette of fuchsia, yellow, blue, orange and others creates a happy and inviting space. The sofa, curtains, and lighting are moderate and joined by items of instinctive colorfulness tending toward kitsch, granting a twist to the design.
Home Styling: Stephanie Gribe. Photography by Uzi Porat.

A home with a concept of joy and renewal, focusing on color and cheerfulness. In the working area, painted boxes reverberate the colors of the chairs, bench, and footrest.

Interior Design: Rona Kenan Fish. Photography by Ora Cohen.

Home Styling: Stephanie Gribe.
Photography by Uzi Porat.
(More on page 148)

Rosh Hashana table inspired
by the tropics with two framed
assemblages and plenty of
flowers and plastic.
Art: Noa Holtzshtein, Tutika

Art: Noa Holtzshein, Tutika

Humorous "linked" sculptures built of vintage porcelain doll heads with vintage dishes, modern plastic and porcelain dishes.

Assemblage inspired by the tropics combined with the face of a vintage doll, plastic fruit and fabric flowers.

ARE YOU COLOR SHY?
Then add just a bit of color to your home.

Neutral colors prevail in Israeli homes and shops. These choices are made by architects and designers, for various reasons ranging from "So you do not get tired of it" and "So your eyes do not hurt" to "We will not manage to sell it." If you are still interested in adding some drops of color, you can do it in small quantities:

- Mix several neutral colors such as white, beige, brown, gray and black.
- Add metallic touches of gold or rose gold to a neutral space.
- Choose colors of a pale pastel version (mint green, light blue) or smoky shades (green or blue mixed with gray).
- Create color spots in the space by means of pictures, cushions, accessories and colorful flowers that may be exchanged by non-expensive buys.

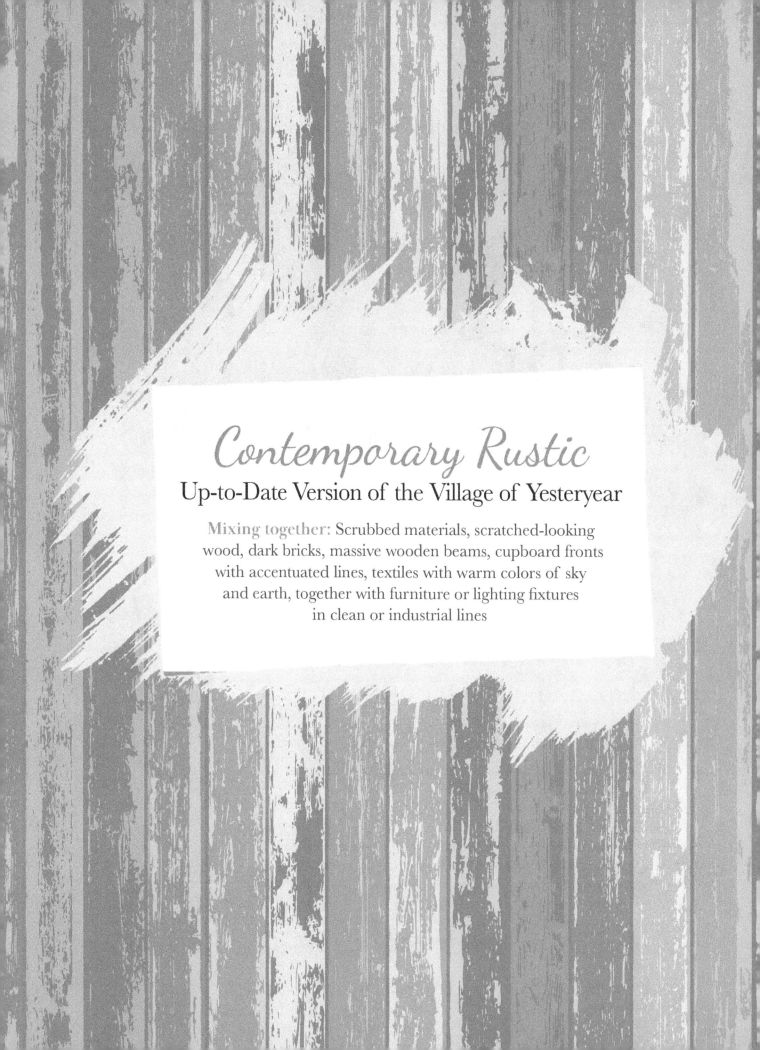

Contemporary Rustic
Up-to-Date Version of the Village of Yesteryear

Mixing together: Scrubbed materials, scratched-looking wood, dark bricks, massive wooden beams, cupboard fronts with accentuated lines, textiles with warm colors of sky and earth, together with furniture or lighting fixtures in clean or industrial lines

A delicate touch of aqua color in the kitchen combined with elements identified with the world of restaurants, such as a kitchen island with drawers, wooden crates and a dining table with a sitting bench.

Architecture and Interior Design: Sara and Nirit Frenkel. Photography by Itay Benit.

Home Styling: Natalie Alal.
Photography by Orit Arnon.

Home Styling: Natalie Alal.
Photography by Orit Arnon.

We have left the modern era and entered the village. Here, the general look is neither clean nor minimalistic, although that may exist as well, as befits the Israeli mixture of styles. What we now have is a modern translation of the village of yesteryear - the elements that are considered rustic blending in with contemporary design. The home provides a warm and pleasant feeling of a village in contemporary regions, with raw and rough lines. There is an increase use of wood, wooden beams, high wooden ceiling, ceiling fans, warm earth colors, cornices, decorated and curving iron hardware, bricks, decorated tiles, free-standing oven, highly detailed lighting fixtures, heavy curtains, accessories from the village and field such as wooden boxes, baskets, enameled pots, straw furniture, and if you can bring some of the plants indoors to feel nature and earth - all the better.

Alongside all of these, completely modern features live in peace. These may be industrial, such as thin legged chairs and side-tables, clean-looking marble, exposed air-condition ducts, clean-lined sofas, etc. Because in real life, village-dwellers also know what modernity is.

Clean lines and and a symmetry maintaining in the home, with an exposed wooden roof and a wall of dismantled bricks, create a feeling that the wall cuts the roof. The black kitchen produces roughness and intensifies the urban sense, and the barn doors reverberate a rustic style. Black aluminum windows complement the essence of the design. *Interior Design: Moli Ben Aharon. Photography by Maor Moyal.*

An open, inviting and soft space that affords movement in it. To intensify the sense of flow, light colors were chosen, warm and soft, wooden tables in the living room and kitchen, and gray-ish beige bricks, imbuing warmth in the home and complementing the monochromatic colors.

Interior Design: Shlomit Gliks.

Photography by Oded Smadar.

A home overlooking a wild green valley, planned with a connection to nature through large openings and natural materials such as stone flooring, dismantled bricks, iron and wood. Contemporary touches of color in the textile, furniture and art intensify the feeling of wildness and the unpredictable aspect of nature. *Interior Design: Shlomit Gliks. Photography by Aviad Bar-Ness.*

A kitchen in an apartment designed in an urban style, with cappuccino-colored solid wood cupboards and a showcase cupboard with laced glass. The kitchen island is covered with a butcher surface of rustic-looking solid wood, and around it white stools. The stainless steel electric items complement the polished look.

Interior Design: Orna Puritz. Photography by Elad Gonen.

The elements that are considered rustic blending in with contemporary design.

A home on a farm with an entirely open high space, balanced by furniture, materials and colors. Dark, dominant wood on the floor and ceiling has supposedly reduced the sense of size and has led to the choice of a light and pleasant-looking color palette. The dramatic living room deep in the home is inviting and elegant with modern lighting fixtures and a low gallery surrounding the light reading area.
Architecture and Interior Design: Alon Cohen. Photography by Shai Epstein.

In the harmonious and inviting living-room, the wooden ceiling beams are painted white. There is a long sofa, a bench for sitting and storage, and armchairs of decorative fabric, adding to the play of textures. An ochre-colored carpet gives a shot of energy, while around it, the off-white of the curtains and ornamental objects imbue a pleasant calm atmosphere.
Interior Design: Bella Yekutiel.
Photography by Lior Torem on behalf of Hardoor.

A gray brick covering and transparent entrance door, leading
to a warm home with parquet floors and wooden furniture.
Architecture and Interior Design: Sara and Nirit Frenkel.
Photography by Itay Benit.

A living room in a Tuscany-inspired home, with natural parquet floor in smoked brown and windows divided by black iron profiles.
Architecture and Interior Design: Sara and Nirit Frenkel.
Photography by Gilad Radat.

A private home with poor light orientations that was renovated and the previous kitchen was left. The home is illuminated by vivid and more natural hues as well as artificial lighting. The kitchen island's surface was replaced with a shiny natural wood to reflect light, and bright lighting fixtures sparkle even when the light is off. The carpentry unit hanging to the left of the island is emphasized with color and the bar chairs connect the wooden island surface, the marble and black handles that were left in the kitchen.

Interior Design: Inbar Menaged.
Photography by Elad Gonen.

Dismantled bricks in a modern kitchen.
Home Styling: Natalie Alal.
Photography by Orit Arnon.

CONTEMPORARY RUSTIC DESIGN –
Where We Can Find It

We have chosen five leading rustic design shops, that also reside in villages, to complete the atmosphere: Turkiz Beit Yitzhak, Turkiz House, Muscat, Ha'asam, and Back Yard. As far as the two sisters of Turkiz are concerned, they are more than just shops, since they include rustic design domains in the Sharon villages. There you can find the washed and unfinished furniture, ornamental tiles and decorated bathroom features, lighting fixtures dismantled from ships that have ended their voyages, or baskets filled with real-looking field flowers. Each of them has a garden area for outdoor furniture, charming sitting corners, an abundance of ideas for bedrooms, kitchens and living rooms, and in Beit Yitzhak - you can even find a chic café for a snack or for dining. The fourth shop, Ha'asam (granary), at the entrance to Kibbutz Kiryat Anavim on the way to Jerusalem, is similar in character - an enormous shop with designed areas, some rustic and some bordering on industrial. The fifth, Back Yard, is in American country style, and all of the furniture and items arrive there after the owners have toured markets and merchant hangars in the USA.

Addresses: Turkiz Beit Yitzhak, 19 Hefer Rd. Beit Yitzhak; Turkiz House, Bnei Dror moshav ;Muscat, Hadekel St. Udim; Ha'asam, Kibbutz Kiryat Anavim; Back Yard, Mashtelat Yahali route 65, Pardes Hanna-Karkur Junction.

Cosmic Softness

Floating among the Clouds

Mixing together: White color, pastel colors,
white curtains, gently carved items and lighting fixtures,
rustic romantic lighting fixtures made of glass, furniture
with delicate forms and carved elements as well
as soft looking textiles.

A room inspired by a European styled hotel with pink cornices for a classic elegant feeling.
Dramatic blue bed upholstery balanced by side tables, Carrera marble surfaces, and brass
legs, a woolen carpet for a feeling of softness and an armchair upholstered in light fur.
Interior Design and Home Styling: Liron Otmazgin, Studio Adida. Photography by Shai Epstein.

An apartment facing the sea with soft romantic materials and colors such as fabrics in hues of pink and purple, walnut for a warm European atmosphere and brass lighting that creates a warm, embracing atmosphere. In addition, there are materials that are stiffer and more modern, such as shiny flooring and plant pots which create contrast and interest. In the dining area a painting in similar colors and a black frame. Natural and artificial plants give a sense of renewal, joy and growth. Combined, a sense of harmony is maintained in the warm, inviting and embracing space.
Home Styling: Natalie Alal. Photography by Orit Arnon

Authentic Mediterranean touches, delicate and saucy in a home overlooking a Galilee view, with soft colorful surprises in lamps and furniture.
Interior Design: Merav Zohar. Photography by Shiran Carmel.

This style is just like its name - gentle, tender, delicate, charming its residents and viewers with the prevalent use of white walls, textile and built in furniture, as if one were floating among soft, white and wooly clouds. But not all is white in the kingdom of soft magic. There are touches of pastels such as pink, light blue, banana yellow and wood in quantities that do not exceed the whiteness, thereby leaving it the lion's share of the design. Even if the style contains colors, they are just light or pastel spots in a sea of serenity.

The style of Cosmic Softness uses motifs ranging from light rustic to warm Nordic, for instance in kitchens that are inspired by rustic lines or light modern furniture. However, the language in general is very gentle and light, and on the scale of masculinity to femininity - the blush wins.

A classic and timeless space, well-illuminated and open with a delicate soft hue of coffee and accompanied by plenty of white light to complete the atmosphere.Natural materials such as wood, iron and plants preserve a timeless atmosphere.
Interior Design and Home Styling: Ori Ifrah.
Photography by Noya Shiloni-Haviv.

There are touches of pastels in quantities that do not exceed the whiteness, thereby leaving it the lion's share of the design.

An eclectic, calm and romantic bedroom in the natural hue of sage green with textile in light cream and powder. There is a macramé hanging on the wall with a matching carpet.
Home Styling: Vital Peri Shilton. Photography by Orit Arnon.

A large mint-green circle catches the eye when entering the girl's room. In addition to being a symbol of infinity, it also symbolizes flow and continuity, and therefore was chosen as the central motif. To maintain its totality, the hanging shelf was painted the same color and integrated into it.
Interior Design: Limor Oren. Photography by Orit Arnon.

Window openings enlarged in the home of an amateur pastry chef and painted white for an airy, well-illuminated look as well as emphasizing the light blue of the kitchen. *Interior Design: Carmit Gat. Photography by Itay Benit.*

A rustic design with modern touches create a sense of space in a roof apartment. The dining area has a covering of silicate bricks, and the public space combines furniture and sentimental vintage objects that the family has collected over the years: living room tables from old authentic wine barrels, a vintage pendulum clock from their parents' home, an old wine bar renovated in turquoise with scrubbing that exposes the wood, and hand-made macramé.
Interior Design: Eti Lev Katz. Home styling: Mirit Fich.
Photography by Orit Arnon.

A bedroom with a luxurious and elegant atmosphere while also warm and calm, where light gray hues combine with touches of white and pink. The furniture is a mixture of modern style with rustic carpentry items.
Architecture and Interior Design: Yaara Krakover.
Photography by Elad Gonen.

A scale of light and delicate pinks and blues, greens and smoked grays in the public space reflect the owners' pleasant, calm and harmonious apartment.

Interior Design: Sivan Konvalina. Photography by Orit Arnon.

An apartment in a building for conservation, designed in a romantic eclectic style with a sky blue kitchen, a collection of vintage plates near original wooden windows, a white iron lighting fixture above the island, and ornamental tiles decorating the floor.
Interior Design: Perri Interior Design.
Photography by Shay Epstein.

A contemporary design with a clean, effortless look. Use of quiet colors, the lack of symmetry and a combination of old refurbished furniture with new accessories create interest. Natural materials such as bamboo and cork together with wood and iron add warmth.

Interior Design: Michal Wolfson. Photography by Dana Stempler Asael.

A living room in pastels inspired by a floral wall print of a girl. The vintage-looking coffee table joins the authentic work unit from the 50s that was renovated and suited to the space. A light blue full carpet, vintage style, adds a soft and pleasant texture.
Home Styling and Photography by Limor Kohler.

A home of music lovers with floating stairs made of natural wood and thin, iron strings reminiscent of harp strings, creating movement and harmony. The furniture, textile and ornamental objects have a delicate, reserved classic look and the colors are moderate, like a soft melody.

Interior Design: Anat Hadas. Photography by Orit Arnon.

A children's room with a soft soothing color palette, granting a calm environment together with bookshelves, a PVC illustrated rug, and a wooden table and dresser. A black chalk board encourages artistic expression.
Home Styling: Roni Erlich. Photography by Dana Stempler Asael.

A calm and enveloping home with a caressing softness that embraces and is fun to be in. The choice of pink symbolizing femininity gives a feeling of softness, love, containing sensitivity and cleanliness. The blue expresses good communication, openness, lack of boundaries, flow and learning. The dining table is comfortable to convene around, and the living room has modular and dynamic units enabling easy change. The play of textile creates a soft feeling, interesting and sophisticated.

Interior Design: Adi Kedmi. Photography by Shai Epstein.

Vintage and Nordic elements in a couple's apartment. Rich textile of a pleasant and pampering Berber carpet and a buffet from the 50s imbue warmth, charm and character into the space with calm colors. The calm and warm atmosphere is preserved in the bedroom by a wall painted green and warm textile.

Interior Design and Home Styling: Revital Erez. Photography by Orit Arnon.

WALKING
between
THE GENDERS

Cosmic Softness, due to its name and from the pictures and definitions of this style, is almost immediately affiliated to feminine softness. Is it possible to design a masculine or feminine space? Or is the definition of such a space the result of stereotypes? This has long been debated, but we will provide several of the features supposedly differentiating between the genders, and leave the decision to the readers' judgment. We will only mention again that most of the rooms are in any case a mixture of features from here and from there:

Pastel colors, cream and natural, pinks, purples and mainly soft or faded colors are attributed to "feminine design" while the dark colors, particularly gray, black and brown - to men.

Round shapes, less geometric, as well as floral elements are favorites for the feminine side.

Botanical patterns, dots and other decorative elements are considered feminine, while stripes, checkered and fishbone are considered masculine.

Materials such as gold, marble and crystal tend to the feminine side, while iron, leather, and rough elements are affiliated to the masculine one.

Accessories, romantic lamps, cushions and textile mainly decorate feminine spaces, while their minimal use is affiliated with masculine spaces.

Multi-Layered Warm White

Minimalism Does not Live Here

Mixing together: White color, layers of white, rich textures, rough materials, natural motifs such as plants, straw, rich styling.

A white kitchen that mixes classic and warm rustic, with a wooden butcher surface and porcelain granite tiling with a medallion-patterned vintage look.
Architecture and Interior Design: Moshik Hadida. Photography by Oded Smadar.

A pampering and calm apartment with a sense of freedom, where monochromatic hues are joined by delicate touches of green and gold. The materials and textures create interest and character, matching the owner's field of creation and art. The bricks are dirty-white, the kitchen is cream color mixed with white, combined with oak wood on the island's surface and the shelves. Touches of gold on the lighting fixtures, accessories, handles and iron hardware add glitter and style.

Interior Design and Home Styling: Yifat Abramson. Photography by Shiran Carmel.

Interior Design and Home Styling:
Yifat Abramson.
Photography by Shiran Carmel.

Almost like the cosmic whiteness of the Cosmic Softness style, in this style as well the white color plays a central role, but you will not find softness or a floating sensation here. Rather - there is a mixture of layers of textures that create a full, warm look, far from minimalistic.

The white color is seemingly anemic, emitting coldness. Many choose it not only for the cold modern style but for other styles as well, even people tending toward the rustic style so identify with the colors of wood. In this specific style, which we have defined as Multi-Layered Warm White, the textures and materials are rich due to the layers of white elements. The materials are found in various shapes. They may look massive or have a rough texture, such as white bricks or wooden beams painted white. They may combine black wrought-iron works, dark furniture, gray grout between white tiles, a moderate quantity of wood or natural motifs warming up the atmosphere, such as straw, plants, and stylized ornamented items.

The styling does not leave empty spaces and minimalism is not part of it. In this category we can find a modern look, rustic, Nordic or industrial - but all rendered unique by the total use of white, and the ability to warm up the view with a variety of aids, as well as filling the space with textural abundance. To sum it up, if it is not white, it does not belong here.

A white kitchen, located between the external wall and the staircase, creates a sense of space and tranquility. The concrete tiles are in black and white. The white-framed openings bring the outdoors in.

Architecture and Interior Design: Adi Amit Freiman. Photography by Aviv Kurt.

200

The use of white walls and a wooden floor creates a warm light and well-illuminated space in the open kitchen. Delicate touches of wood and color in the lighting fixtures break the monochrome scale. *Architecture and interior design: Adi Amit Freiman. Photography by Aviv Kurt.*

201

A kitchen connecting the rustic with clean contemporary
lines with the use of bricks, stone and stainless steel.
Architecture and Interior Design: Sara and Nirit Frenkel.
Photography by Gilad Radat.

In this specific style the textures and materials are rich due to the layers of white elements. The materials are found in various shapes.

An escapist space where one can feel a real detachment as in
a pampering vacation. With richness of white hues, warmth of
a rough parquet, and touches of green from outdoors evoke a
particularly soothing ambiance.
Architecture and Interior Design: Shira Muskal and Hadas Roth,
Halel Studio. Photography by Oded Smadar.

A room imbuing calmness and pampering, with a big white bed, soft and inviting, soft curtains and a white-beamed ceiling, connecting together in harmony for a restful experience.

Architecture and Interior Design: Shira Muskal and Hadas Roth, Halel Studio. Photography by Oded Smadar.

A white kitchen, the heart of the home, where the family convenes around a central island. Open shelves serve for the everyday dishes. Ornamental objects and plants add charm and beauty.
Interior Design: Limor Oren. Photography by Orit Arnon.

A kitchen with an old and rough surfaced dining table and antiquated and renovated chairs. The flooring is painted Moroccan tiles, the aluminum windows are densely divided, and the cupboards are Provence carpentry tying the elements together in harmony.

Architecture and Interior Design: Lirane Benivgi, Lev architecture.
Photography by Idan Goor.

A home in monochromatic colors of gray and white is granted warmth by natural materials such as natural wood, Provence-style kitchen cupboards and exposed beams on the ceiling. Windows of white iron profiles, constructed according to the roof's slopes, introduce the garden into the home.

Architecture and Interior Design: Lirane Benivgi, Lev architecture.
Photography by Idan Goor.

A bathroom with the look of a clean and immaculate spa, where white has a major role. The design is timeless, classic and pleasant created by subway tiles and windows of thin white steel profiles with frosted glass that introduce light while maintaining privacy. The cupboard and mirror produce a surprise that does not belong to the world of water, and the black floor serves to contrast and accentuate the presence of white.

Interior Design: Inbar Kerper-Saranovitz. Photography by Nadav Peket.

A home creating a sense of freedom and warmth inspired by homes in Greece and in the Hamptons. The colorfulness is soothing, based on delicate, light and calm colors. The kitchen has two sitting areas inviting the outdoors in.
Architecture: Sharon Weiser. Photography by Oded Smadar.

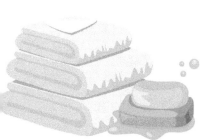

A home exemplifying a European concept, with wooden columns 5.5 meters high and a modern fireplace up to the ceiling and covered in bricks. Natural materials were chosen for the home, such as polished stone for the floor, solid wood for the kitchen, and a knights' table in the dining area. White was chosen in order to create a warm, pleasant and timeless feeling.
Interior Design: Shirly Dan. Photography by Yoav Peled / Peled Studios.

A parents' suite with the feeling of a holiday place and windows looking out to the pool in the yard. Exposed white wooden beams emphasize the space's height. The white parquet floor and brick wall complement the ambiance.
Interior Design: Shirly Dan. Photography by Shay Adam.

A white kitchen with an eclectic combination of materials such as wood, iron, metal and the play of black and white with touches of green. The white tiles are accentuated by gray grout, and the open shelves are useful while adding style and contemporary chic.

The play of black and white in the bathroom lend a clean look, with a white laundry cupboard, black and white tiles and the white brick covering emphasized by gray grout. The delicate wall plastering in stone color, frames the space.

Interior Design: Dikla Glazer. Photography by Shiran Carmel.

HOW DOES THE WHITE CONNECT
to Warmth and to the Office?

The Multi-Layered Warm White style can also be applied to offices. In the architecture and interior design firm of Sara and Nirit Frenkel, they remodeled the office while creating a relaxed working area reflecting a homey and familial concept of design, befitting a mother and daughter working together. The space has only one direction of light, and therefore the white color prevails in the space, reflecting light and making the space look larger. In order to achieve a layered look, layers of textures and materials were constructed with a whitened wooden ceiling, bricks colored white, a parquet, and screens of light-colored carpentry inlaid with glass. The glass mass creates an airy feeling, enabling the light to inundate the rest of the spaces.

Architecture and Interior Design: Sara and Nirit Frenkel. Photography by Itay Benit.

Afterword

Of the scores of contemporary styles, we have
 chosen ten styles that are the essence of a vibrant
developing country, in a field that is exciting and
changing, affected from all over the globe, and
always on the watch for something new.
There is no telling what it will be like tomorrow.
Life is dynamic, with continuous changes, so we
may very quickly have material for another book.
As always, time will tell.